Tying the Knot

Remembering Our Wedding

havoc
PUBLISHING

© 1997 Havoc Publishing

ISBN 1-57977-102-5

Published and created by Havoc Publishing

San Diego, California

First Printing, May 1997

Some images © 1997 PhotoDisc, Inc.

Printed in China

Designed by Juddesign

Please write to us for more information on our
Havoc Publishing Record Books and Products.

HAVOC PUBLISHING
9808 Waples Street,
San Diego, CA 92121

Tying the Knot

Remembering Our Wedding

This book records the wedding of

Contents

The Proposal & Pre-Wedding Celebrations

About the Bride & About the Groom

Our New Family Tree

Photographs

The Showers & Parties

The Rehearsal Dinner

The Announcement & Invitation

Photographs

The Dress, Shoes & Veil

Time to Primp

Photographs

Memorable Headaches

Something Old, Something New

Tying the Knot

Contents

The Wedding Party

Photographs

It's Legal!

Kisses, Toasts & Dances

Eventful Happenings

Resources

Photographs

Special Times

Photographs

Our First Night

The Gifts

Gift List

The Honeymoon

And So It All Began

The Proposal

Will you marry me?

When

_____

Where

_____

_____

_____

How

_____

_____

He said

_____

_____

_____

She said

_____

_____

_____

Pre Wedding Celebrations

When

Engagement Gifts

From   Gift

_____

Where

_____

Who attended

About the Bride

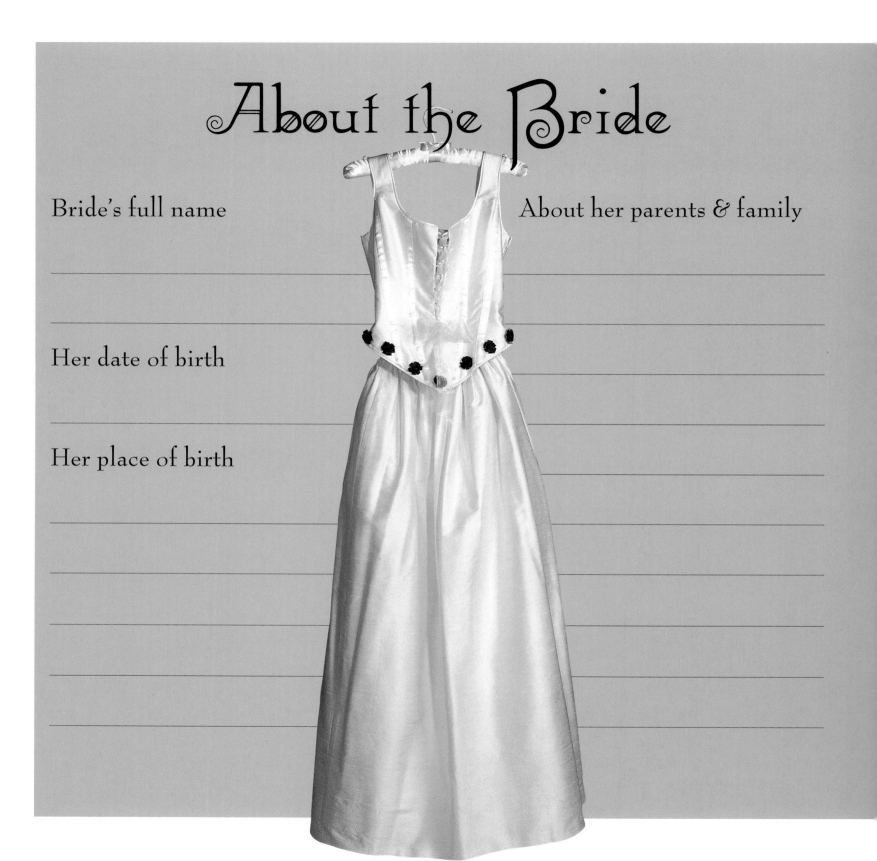

Bride's full name

_____

_____

Her date of birth

_____

Her place of birth

_____

_____

_____

_____

About her parents & family

_____

_____

_____

_____

About the Groom

Groom's full name

_____

_____

His date of birth

_____

His place of birth

_____

_____

_____

About his parents & family

_____

_____

_____

_____

_____

_____

Our New Family Tree

 His  Hers

Parents

Parents

Sisters/Brothers

Sisters/Brothers

Maternal Grandparents

Maternal Grandparents

Paternal Grandparents

Paternal Grandparents

Photograph

The Shower

Who came

_____

_____

_____

_____

Date

_____

Place

_____

Given by

_____

Gifts

_____

_____

_____

_____

Parties

Bachelor party

_____

_____

_____

_____

_____

_____

_____

Bachelorette party

_____

_____

_____

_____

_____

_____

_____

A HAPPY LOT
AWAITS YOU
IN MATRIMONY.

The Rehearsal

Location
_____

Date and time
_____

_____

What we did
_____

_____

_____

Special guests
_____

_____

The menu
_____
_____
_____
_____
_____
_____

Dinner

Special toasts & quotes
_____
_____
_____

Memorable moments
_____
_____
_____
_____

You're Invited!

How many people came

How many people on the bride's side

How many people on the groom's side

Who traveled the farthest to attend

Newspaper clippings
or other notes

The Invitation

place invitation here

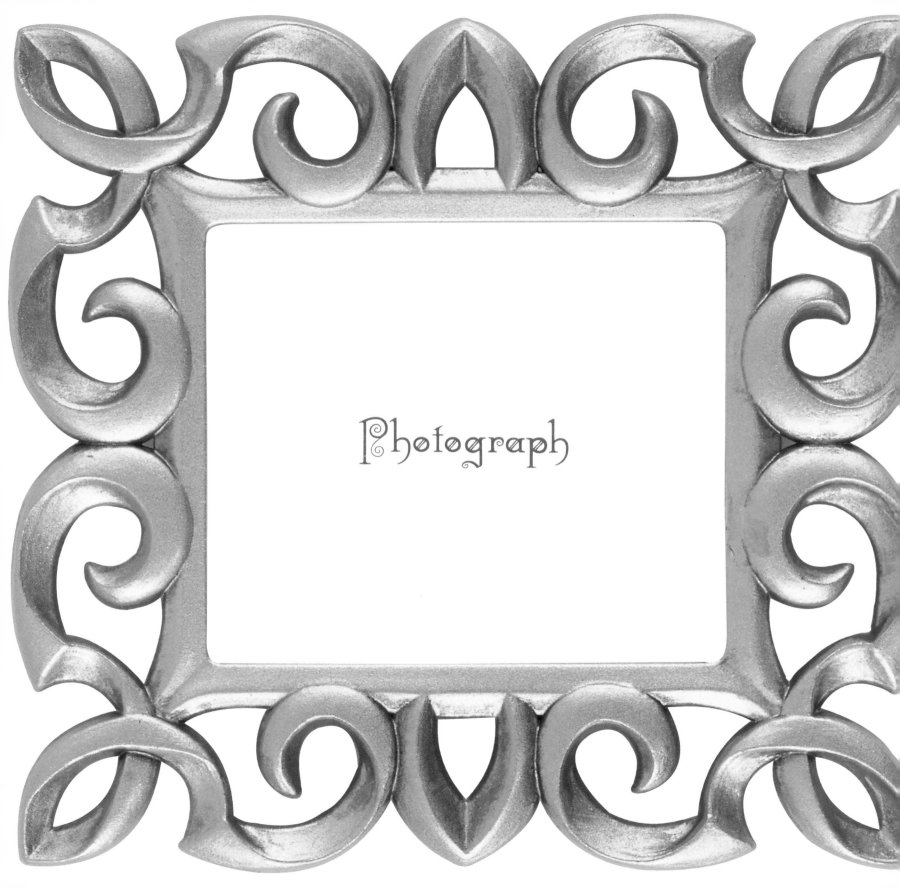

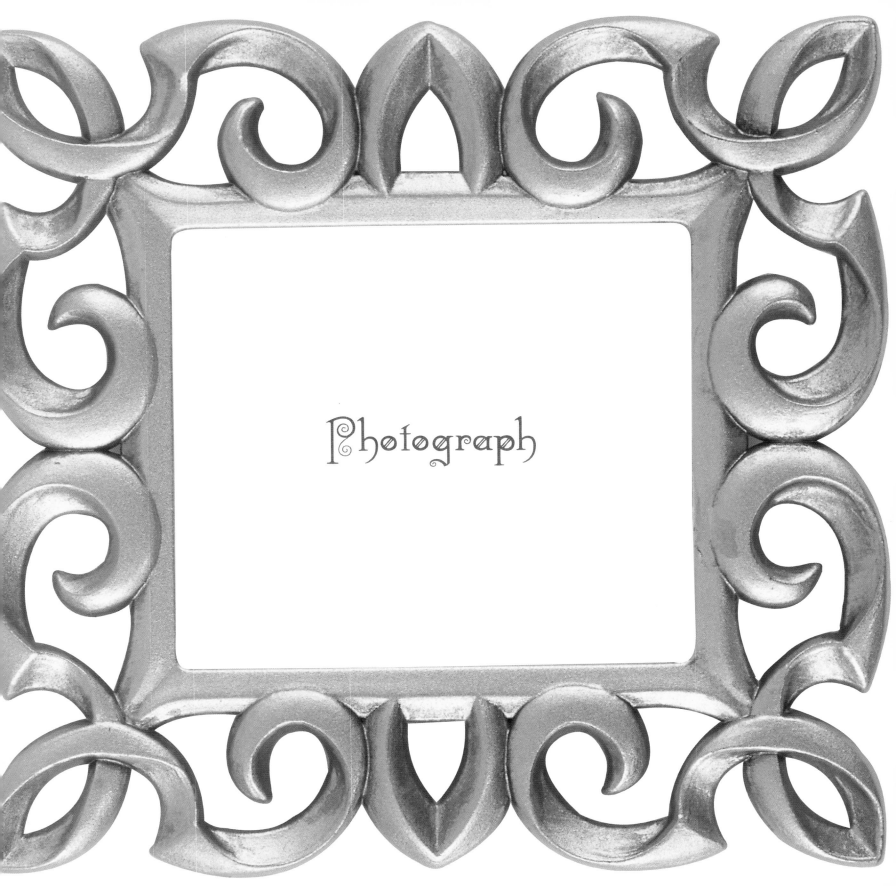

Photograph

Photo of dress

The Dress, Shoes & Veil

My dress _____

Style _____

_____

Fabric _____

_____

Designer _____

Where I bought it _____

_____

Who went with me _____

_____

Shoes _____

_____

Veil _____

_____

Jewelry _____

_____

Garter _____

Undergarments _____

_____

Other special items _____

Time to Primp

Hair stylist
_____

How I wore my hair
_____

_____

_____

_____

Massage and facial

_____

_____

_____

_____

_____

_____

Nails and make-up

_____

_____

_____

What I did to pamper myself

_____

_____

Photograph

Photograph

Memorable

_____

_____

_____

_____

_____

_____

_____

_____

Headaches

_____

_____

_____

_____

_____

_____

_____

Something Old

Something New

Something Borrowed

Something Blue

Tying the Knot

Date & time

Location

Description of the facility

Weather that day

Who presented the bride

Type of ceremony

Who married us

Processional music

Recessional music

Witnesses

The Bride
and her attendants

Maid/Matron of Honor
_____

_____

Bridesmaids
_____

_____

_____

_____

_____

_____

_____

_____

Personal attendants
_____

_____

Flower girl
_____

What they wore
_____

_____

Gifts from the bride
_____

_____

_____

The Groom
and his men

Best man

_____

_____

Groomsmen

_____

Ushers

_____

_____

Ring bearer

_____

What they wore

Gifts from the groom

Photograph

It's Legal!

The Marriage License

...ON FOR LICENSE TO MARRY

...nd Safety Code, Section 10004 and 10675).
...ill result in a license not being issued.

Please Note: All items must...
Refusal or failure to provide complete...

PLEASE PRINT

GROOM

Name:
First: _____
Middle: _____
Last: _____

Date of Birth: _____

Residence:
Address: _____
City: _____
Zip code: _____
County: _____
State/Country of Birth: _____
Mailing Address: _____

Number of Previous Marriages: _____

Last Marriage Ended By:
[ ]Death [ ]Divorce [ ]Annulment

Date Marriage Ended: _____

Usual Occupation: _____

Kind of Business: _____

Highest School Grade or College Completed: _____

Father's
Full name: _____
State of Birth: _____

Mother's Full
Maiden name: _____
State of Birth: _____

Groom: Home Phone: (___)___-___
Work Phone: (___)___-___

BRIDE

Name:
First: _____
Middle: _____
Current Last: _____
Maiden: _____
Date of Birth: _____

Residence:
Address: _____
City: _____
Zip code: _____
County: _____
State/Country of Birth: _____
Mailing Address: _____

Number of Previous Marriages: _____

Last Marriage Ended By:
[ ]Death [ ]Divorce [ ]Annulment

Date Marriage Ended: _____

Usual Occupation: _____

Kind of Business: _____

Highest School Grade or College Completed _____

Father's
Full name: _____
State of Birth: _____

Mother's Full
Maiden name: _____
State of Birth: _____

Bride: Home Phone: (___)___-___
Work Phone: (___)___-___

Marriage Certificate

Kisses, Toasts & Dances
(The Reception)

Where

When

Program

Toasts & Speeches

Best man

Others

Favorite quotes

2.

1.

Song for first dance

Why we chose that song

Other favorite tunes

Father/Daughter dance

Mother/Son dance

The Cake

Flavor

_____

Number of tiers

_____

Bakery

_____

Photo of cake

Eventful Happenings

Who caught the bouquet

_____

Who caught the garter

_____

Favors of the reception

_____

_____

_____

Caterer

Name _____

Menu _____

_____

_____

_____

_____

_____

_____

_____

Music

Name _____

Favorite music _____

_____

_____

_____

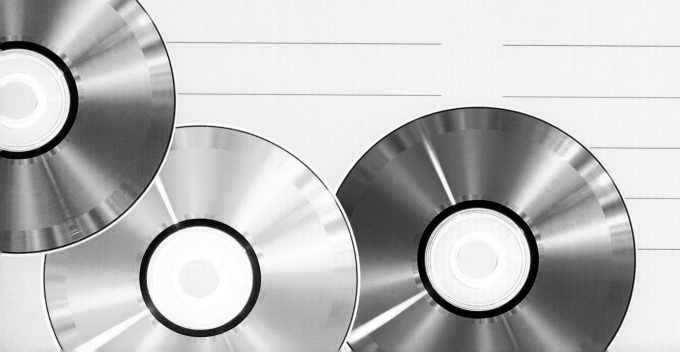

Photographer

Name _____

Videographer

Name _____

Florist

Name _____

Type of flowers _____

_____

_____

_____

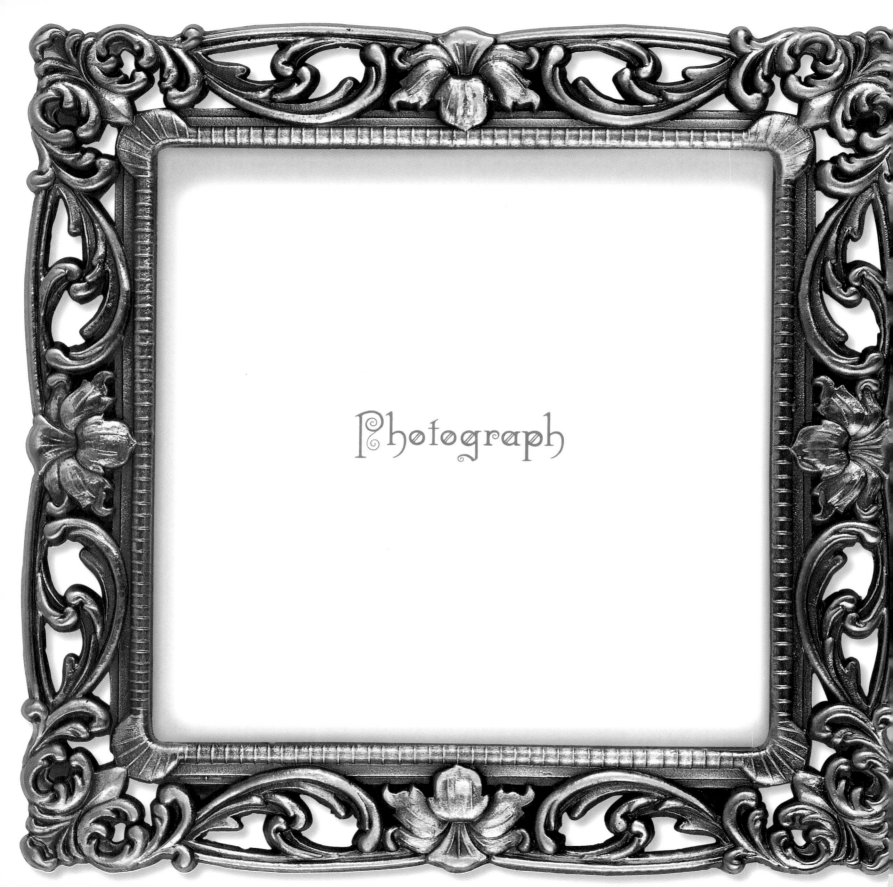

Special Times,
Funny Moments

Surprises

Candid photo

Candid photo

Photograph

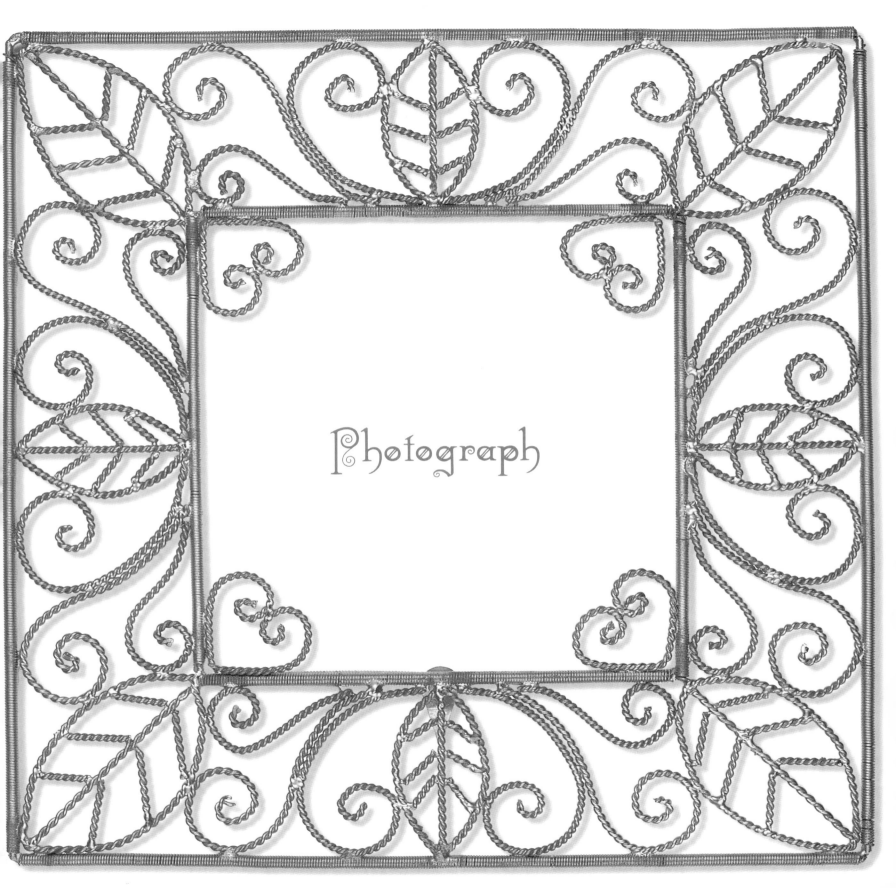

Do
Not
Disturb!

Our First Night

What time we left the reception
_____

Where we spent the night
_____

Thoughts of the evening
_____

_____

_____

_____

Special memories
_____

_____

_____

The Gifts

Our gifts to each other

_____

_____

_____

Favorite gifts

_____

_____

_____

Funniest gifts

_____

_____

Most unusual gifts

_____

_____

_____

Most duplicate gifts

_____

_____

_____

From   Gift

The Honeymoon

Dates of honeymoon

_____

_____

Where we went

_____

_____

Where we stayed

_____

_____

Our favorite restaurants

_____

_____

Our favorite places

_____

_____

_____

Our special memories

_____

_____

_____

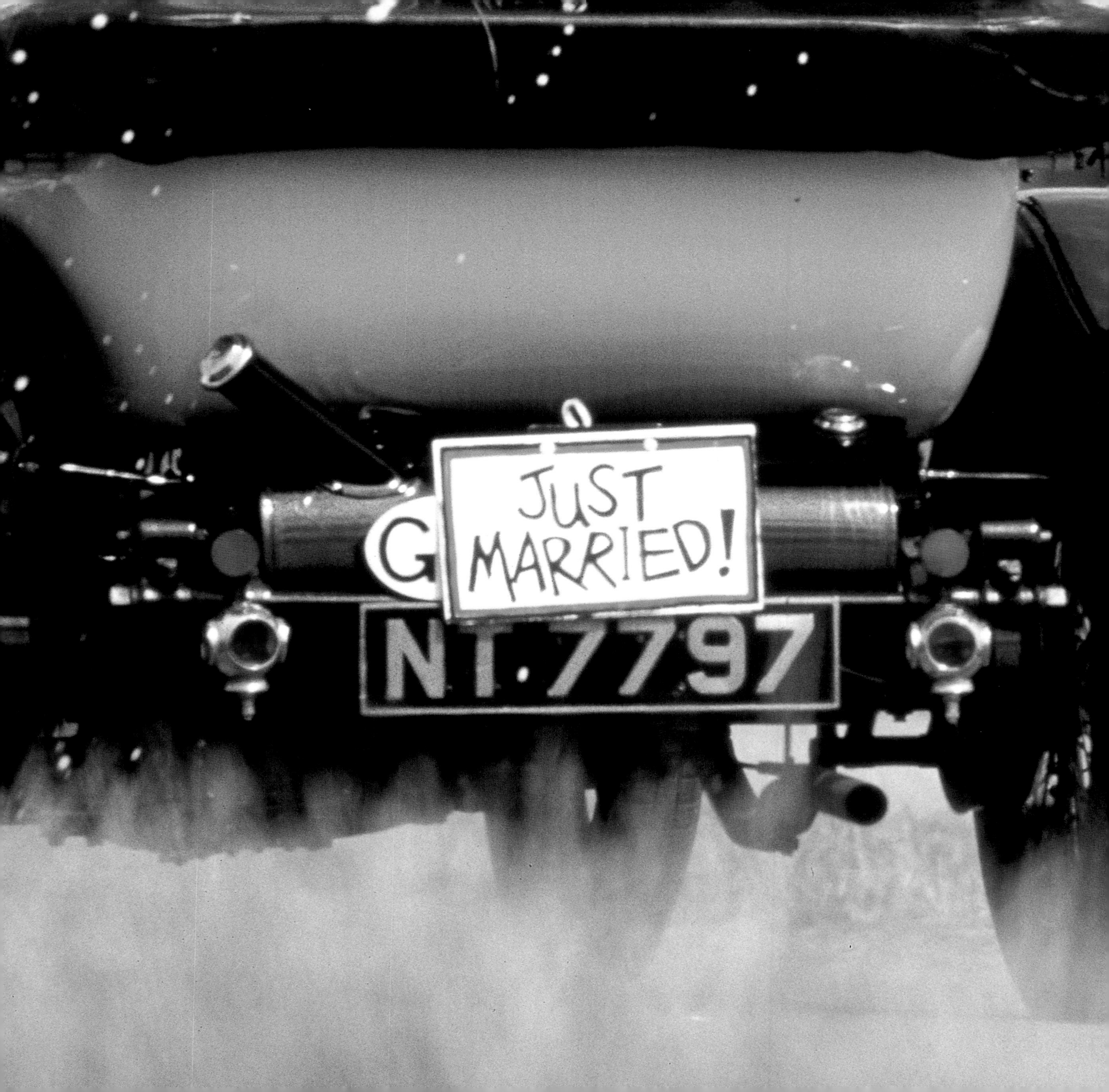
JUST MARRIED!
G
NT 7797

Photograph

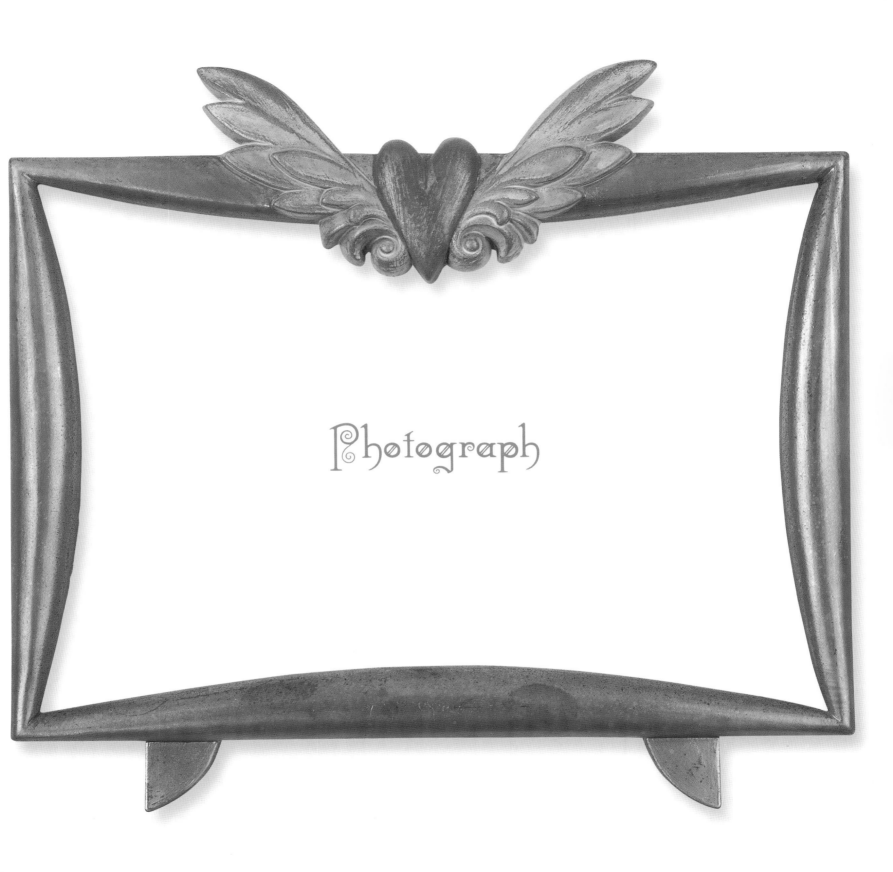

Photograph

His

Hers

And So It All Began...

Mr. & Mrs.

_____

Our new address

_____

_____

_____

Available Record Books
from Havoc

Animal Antics - Cats

Animal Antics - Dogs

Couples

Girlfriends

Golf

Grandmother

Our Honeymoon

Mom

Sisters

Tying the Knot

Traveling Adventures

Please write to us with your ideas for additional
Havoc Publishing Record Books and Products

HAVOC PUBLISHING
9808 Waples Street,
San Diego, CA 92121